If I Were A...
POLICE OFFICER

The adventure of policework in pictures!

NorthParadePublishing

Published in 2010 by North Parade Publishing Ltd.
4 North Parade
Bath
BA1 1LF
UK

If I Were A...
POLICE OFFICER
The adventure of policework in pictures!

INTRODUCTION

Most children are probably familiar with the police officer, but how much do they know about this important community helper?

This book is a pictorial journey through the world of the police officer. An easy read book for children, it acquaints children with the various activities that police officers engage in.

The pictures in the book have been carefully selected for the range of important police work they display.

The brief, bite-sized text is designed for easy reading by the early reader to compliment the photography.

Police officers have to be ever ready to maintain law and order. It is also their job to help people who are in trouble.

Some police officers travel in cars and on motorbikes and scooters. A few lucky ones get to ride horses, sometimes even camels. They are called the mounted police.

Some police officers move around on bicycles. These people can reach places where bigger vehicles cannot reach.

In many countries there are special forces to patrol the highways. They see to it that people drive within the speed limit. They also help out if there is an accident.

Even the military has its own police force. These police officers make sure that people in the military follow the rules and don't break the law.

Some police officers are there to make sure that the traffic on the roads flows smoothly. They are known as the traffic police.

It is the job of traffic police officers to control traffic. They have to guide the flow of vehicles and prevent people from breaking road rules.

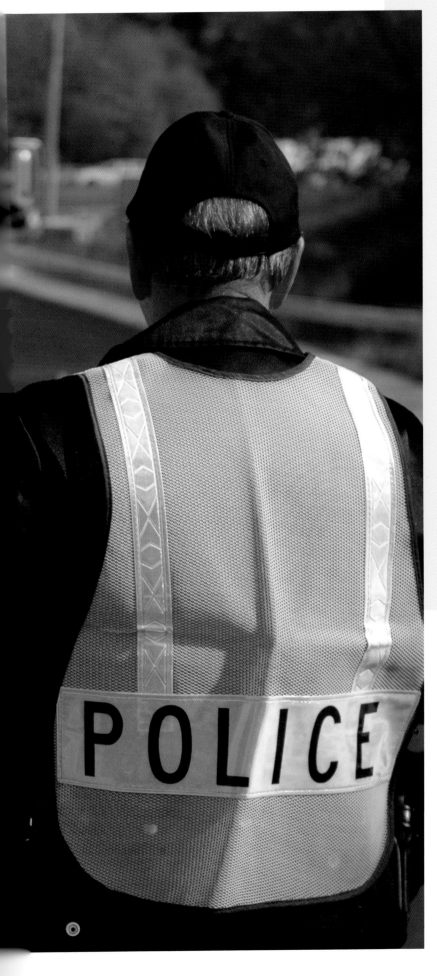

Traffic police officers work in a very dangerous location, in the middle of the road. So they wear bright yellow jackets so that they are visible at all times.

Traffic police officers keep in constant touch with their colleagues in the control rooms.

Street cameras everywere
help to track any violations
taking place on the road.

The police officer's job is not easy. They have to be vigilant and careful all the time. The safety of a lot of people depends on them.

A police officer has to uphold the law and be prepared to be firm but fair with those who break it.

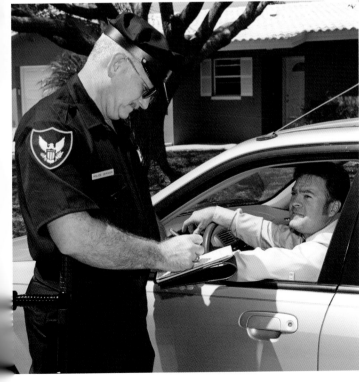

Sometimes members of
the police force take part
in parades held in towns
or cities and people gather
as they pass by on their
gleaming vehicles.

Police officers are called in when the crowds get too rowdy and people start rioting. When the crowds are large and violent the police sometimes have to use force.

These police officers
have special protective
shields and body armour
to protect them in the
event of a riot.

When an accident occurs, the police are usually the first to reach the scene. They help the people involved and direct traffic, as well as making the scene safe.

It is not easy to become a police officer. One has to undergo a lot of intense training. This training can run for several months.

An essential part of training for armed police, is learning how to handle a firearm. Some police officers have to be expert marksmen so they don't miss their target if they have to shoot.

Some police officers are involved in helicopter rescue work and have special training for it.

Most of the essential equipment for a police officer is carried on their person, either on their belts or clipped to their shoulder pads.

Police officers use a variety of gadgets and devices to help them handle some of the more dangerous jobs, like this bomb disposal vehicle.

Police officers have to be able to work in all conditions: on land, air, and even on water. After all, emergencies can happen almost anywhere!

Some police forces also have boats which they use to patrol the rivers, harbours and coast line.

Modern police forces also use dogs in some circumstances. Dogs have an excellent sense of smell and can be trained to find things.

Specially trained dog handlers direct the dogs as they sniff a car or a suitcase to tell if there is anything dangerous hidden inside.

Dog handlers usually handle the same dog for a long time and build a special relationship to get the best out of the dog. It's a big responsibility.

When a crime is committed, it is the duty of the police to investigate thoroughly and try to bring those responsible to justice.

Another aspect of policework involves examining the site of a crime and looking for clues that will help solve the crime. This is known as investigating.

Police investigators will examine every inch of a crime scene closely and make a note of everything they find on the scene. Who knows what tiny bit might help solve the crime?

The first thing police officers do at a crime scene is look for fingerprints. The criminal might have touched an object and left their fingerprint on it.

Once they have a fingerprint, they take prints from likely suspects and compare them to the prints at the crime. If they find a match, they know who did the crime.

GLOSSARY

Armour:	a covering worn as a defence against weapons
Arrest:	to catch and hold someone
Clue:	anything that helps to solve a mystery
Colleague:	someone who works with you
Crime:	any activity that breaks the law
Criminal:	someone who commits a crime
Evidence:	anything that helps to prove a crime
Gleaming:	shining brightly
Handcuff:	restrain someone with a ringlike device that locks around the wrist
Highway:	a main road between towns and cities

Investigate:	systematically examining a crime
Law:	rules that govern a society
Outsmart:	think better than someone else
Punish:	apply a penalty to someone for a crime
Riot:	noisy and violent public disorder
Victim:	the person who suffers because of a crime
Vigilant:	watchful
Violate:	break a law
Violent:	causing serious injury and destruction by use of force
Weapon:	any tool used to intimidate or inflict harm on someone